Becoming Beautiful
Encounters with the Truth Teller

Michelle Sims

Copyright © 2016 Michelle Sims

All rights reserved.

ISBN-13: 978-1532945625
ISBN-10: 1532945620

DEDICATION

To Brandon and Caitlin, thank you for always believing in me.
I love you.

CONTENTS

    Acknowledgments

1   An Introduction   1
2   Unexpected Beginnings   5
3   Whispers and Shakings   11
4   Transitions   15
5   Perspective   21
6   Faith Walk   27
7   Becoming Beautiful   35
8   Abiding   49
9   Seeds of Faith   57
10   A Direct Path   61
11   Holy Huddle   65

ACKNOWLEDGMENTS

A few of the amazing family, friends, and pastors that have been a part of my journey:

Jeff, Joel, Josh, Team, Shay, Ryan, Jenny, Deann, Shyra, Laura, Joanne, Kathy, Snetzer, Bonnie, Prayer Team, Sandra, Caroline, Jennifer, Martha, Robert, Cinnamon, Brandon, Natalie, Jesse, Jessica, Holy Spirit, Patti, Jesse, Travis, Brianna, Gretchen, Mom, Michael, Seth, Freeland, Katherine, Joy, Caitlin, Jen, Clarissa, Britney, Sabrina, Da, Collin, Abba, Barbara, Stephen, Clay, Sergio, Albert, Sarah, David, Jason, Julie, Will, Lori, Mark

CHAPTER 1

AN INTRODUCTION

That's weird.
    Could be God.
        Probably is.
            ~Michael "Freeland" Miller

When I heard my pastor make this statement, I laughed out loud. I had not always had that perspective. This book is, in some ways, a recounting of *my journey* to a place of being able to see God's activity in everything, every moment, every breath. In other ways, the stories that follow are about *our common journey*. There is a constant link among followers of Jesus: someone a step ahead reaches back to help you up, even as you reach behind to help a brother or sister. There have been hundreds of people who have given me a "hand up" over the years, and I am extending mine to anyone who may find it a help.

With a mindset to help others, it is probably not a surprise that I found myself serving in a ministry of reconciliation at my church called Recovery and Steps, which focused on walking with people out of some of the darkest places imaginable into life; and into freedom, hope, and deep joy in the Lord

The first time I shared my story at Recovery I focused on my past - how I accepted Christ when I was six, but became angry and embittered with God when He "let" my parents get divorced when I was nine. I detailed how I was harmed by others in ways that crushed any sense of value I had as a human being, as well as my understanding of personal space and boundaries. I shared how my attempt to be valued led me down a path to a very dark life lived trying to make my own hope, while feeling the weight of responsibility for the chaos raging around me that was completely outside my control. Finally, I shared the goodness in how the Lord overcame all that brokenness in my heart, soul, and mind and began to make me whole.

Hindsight may be "20/20," but it took a lot of time, effort and a deeply humbled mind for me to realize that *how* I was hurt and *who* hurt me, really isn't a key to unlocking my story or the inner freedom I now walk in. What happened in my mind, heart, and soul is a result of *my response* to abuse, circumstance, and spiritual oppression. The key to unlocking my story is what the Lord did to change how I *responded* to the life that happened to me.

Over my years in ministry, I walked with hundreds of women pursuing healing and wholeness and found a pattern emerging: the women and I often believed the same lies about ourselves and God's nature and character; however, we got to those misunderstandings by very different routes. As I share some encounters and "a-ha!" moments over the course of 17 years, I will focus on where my own heart and mind were when the Lord reached in and began to shift my understanding from lies to truth. I think we will find common ground there, and my deep hope is that in that common ground, the Lord will begin to reach in and help others experience this type of change as well.

Before I begin to walk through these bits of my story, you should know I have really crazy encounters with the Lord. He is very purposeful and dramatic and works in circles and cycles that make my head spin sometimes. I mention this now for a couple of reasons. First, I am prone to compare, and if you are too, I am asking you not to. Just stick comparison on the shelf as you read the chapters of this book and know that whatever story I have to tell is for the purpose of letting you share in it. These are not my stories; they are God's stories, so they are *our stories*. Second, there are lots of really smart people who have books and blogs on the continuation of the gifts of the Spirit. I am not going use this book to make that case. I do encourage you to believe that God, creator of EVERYTHING out of NOTHING, who knit each of us together, is ABLE to use ALL THIINGS, including our senses, imagination, creation, and other people, to teach us, grow our faith, and conform us into the image of His Son, Jesus. He is ABLE to do this. He WANTS to do this. He knows us perfectly and held nothing back when He gave Himself on the cross. No matter how well you know Him, God wants you to know Him better. God wants deeper intimacy with you and my prayer at this moment is that your heart and mind will be open to receive His pursuit of you. I hope that as you read my story, it will minister to you and ignite a new thing within *you* for *Him*, His kingdom and glory. He works all things together for the good of those that love Him, and, as you will read, He is even good to those that don't love Him- *yet*.

My final encouragement and prayer is that as you read my story you hear the Lord *speaking to you*. Scripture tells us He walked in the garden with Adam and Eve, but today He *dwells within each person* that has called Him Lord. With this indwelling, we are able to hear His voice and know it from any other voice. It takes practice, though. Think about someone you have known a long time and how you can hear them say something in a room full of people and it is distinguished, it stands out; not only the sound but the character. That was not true when you first met. We are also all able to tune out unwanted sound - kids playing in a park, airplanes overhead, and we can tune out the Lord as well. Ask the Lord to help you distinguish His voice. Not only while reading this book, but every moment of every day.

CHAPTER 2

UNEXPECTED BEGINNINGS

Beauty is in the eye of the beholder.

What is the first thought that came to you after reading those words? The quiet little knee-jerk reaction within?

What if I tell you that YOU are beautiful?

Yes, YOU! You are BEAUTIFUL. You are LOVELY.

Our purpose on this earth is hindered until we are able to behold ourselves as our creator does. To see how beautiful in His sight we really are.

That is my purpose. My call. To tell every person I meet, in whatever way the Lord leads me to say it in the moment, who the Lord formed them to be and made alive on the cross.

This is the beginning of my story; my journey, of having my blind eyes opened, or rather, removing the wrong filters from my vision so I can see truth.

Once upon a time the words "I am such a wretched creature" came from my mouth and I meant them with everything in me.

That is how I saw myself. Deformed. Physically unattractive. Never good enough. Never wanted. Barely tolerated by others. Never having any value or worth. A waste of the oxygen I breathed, and a burden on the world around me simply by exhaling.

In stark contrast, those around me saw me as a sort of super woman. I had a very successful career, volunteered in the public schools in officer roles in the parent teacher organization, started ministries at church, ministered to many people each week, and was very knowledgeable about the Bible.

The Lord saw me very differently than either I or the world did.

My journey to see myself as He sees me began the morning of Sunday, July 25, 1999. I hung up the phone and uttered a few expletives as I tried to think of how I would back out of the "YES" I had given when my sister asked me to go to church with her.

Only a year earlier after taking 'extra' Prozac and drinking too much wine I found myself laying on my bathroom floor with paramedics standing over me, pleading with me to let them take me to the emergency room so I wouldn't die. It is the grace of God I recall my response, "Let me die and go to hell, it is better than this place."

While that moment was a very low point, I was even less enthusiastic about life as I scrambled to think of a plausible lie to get out of going to church. I was not interested in being judged by a bunch of perfectly manicured Bible thumpers, but I had come up with nothing by the time my sister arrived at my door. I got into her car quietly and spent my mental and emotional energy on the knot of fear in my gut threatening to make me throw up.

The church was large. I felt intimidated by the responses between those around me.

"How are you today, Joe-Bob?"

"Abundantly blessed! And you?"

"Oh, yes, thankful for every day!"

Who were these people and what universe did they live in?

The ladies were all perfectly dressed; hair styled, clothes ironed, and certainly not smelling of stale cigarettes like I did. It felt like I had been transported into a scene in "Stepford Wives."

The seconds ticked by excruciatingly slow as I walked to a seat in the very back of the big room people were gathering in. Despite my attempts to be invisible, I felt very exposed. As the band began to sing I glanced at what appeared to be a jumbo-tron at the front of the room where a single word jumped out at me.

"Prodigal"

I had no idea what the word meant but as I stared at the large white letters a pressure began to build inside me. The weight of my miserable life was already unbearable, and I felt pressed even further down. Suddenly, I startled myself with my own voice.

"God, if you can possibly still love me, I am done. I can't take another step or breath on my own. I need you to heal every wound going back to when I was a tiny little girl, and break every prison in my heart I have allowed to be created. I am done doing it my way."

I felt a very odd sensation that I have described as "scrubbing bubbles." It started in the tips of my fingers and toes and rushed to the center of my body. I realized tears were dripping from my face and the hair on my arms was standing on end. My mind raced in confusion trying to process what was happening in the core of my being – in my spirit.

What the hell is happening to me and what are people going to think if they see me? I thought.

My mind freaked out, not understanding what was happening to me internally. But all the logic I could muster could not stop my spirit from responding to the Lord that morning.

As suddenly as it began, it ended. I took a deep breath, exhaled slowly, and felt hope for the first time in my life.

I looked back at the jumbo-tron and "prodigal" was still on the screen. The course of my life had changed in a matter of seconds. I had no idea what I was asking when I asked the Lord to heal me. I probably would not have asked for it, if I had.

I had this idea of God being like a genie in a bottle, and was surprised when my life did not instantly turn into sunshine and roses everywhere. I did not know it would take 17 years of the Lord's faithfulness to heal each wound and break every prison as I had asked Him to do.

Looking back over those years I can say without a doubt that I would not have done many things the way the Lord did- but I am glad He did it His way and not mine! He did not simply change my behavior or circumstances, but allowed the fullness of my choices and responses to manifest so that everything I had hope in outside of Him was systematically destroyed. Even as my life unraveled before my eyes, He partnered with me to begin building a solid foundation for me to stand upon.

There were random things I thought I knew about God. I had been to Baptist Sunday School when I was really young, and finished Catholic catechism classes when I was twelve. I felt somewhat "prepared" to be a Christian. I even had a Bible amongst the hundreds of books tucked on shelves around my home. It was a King James Version, and I quickly found myself confused by and cursing at the old English. I decided to buy a Bible I could understand, and discovered the NIV.

It is interesting what memories stick in my mind, as clearly as if they were only a few moments ago. Not knowing where to start, I simply opened my new Bible and began reading. *Jeremiah 31:33* struck me, and I carried it with me as I went back to laundry, dishes, and the office:

"This is the covenant I will make with the people of Israel after that time," declares the LORD. "I will put my law in their minds and write it on their hearts. I will be their God, and they will be my people."

I wanted to be His people. I did not know if this scripture was only for the people of Israel, or included anyone that considered Him their God. I decided I should read the Bible from start to finish to ensure all of its words were 'written' somewhere to some extent in my being.

A hunger for God that I did not understand rose inside me. Things I had heard many times were suddenly understandable.

There were also some weird things happening that I could not explain. I would dismiss them and push aside the fear that rose inside, along with the thought that these odd experiences were evidence I had somehow not fully been saved and still had a foot in the old things I had dabbled in.

You see, I have some unusual gifts that run in my family. My whole life I knew things I had no natural way to know. Saw things no one else saw.

As I got older and sought to understand myself and what was going on, the only readily available information on the supernatural was occult and new age material, so that is what I read.

I probably only qualified as a 'dabbler,' but dabbling opened doors between the natural and supernatural that I had somehow come to believe were only accessed by evil spirits; that Holy Spirit did not interact with us anymore. As a new follower of Jesus, I did not want anything to do with the old spiritual mess. I did not understand that God is the one that wired me the way I am, and did so for His glory. Honestly, I did not even know we could do anything good, much less God-glorifying. I was consumed with keeping the rules and walking a straight line to avoid the wrath of God I believed I still deserved.

Despite my ignorance of Godly supernatural gifts, the weird stuff kept happening. I began to notice that the experiences gave me better understanding of God, and grew my love for Him, and my desire to be like Him. However, I could not shake the fear that somehow, all the unexplainable in my life, meant that I had not really been saved into the Kingdom of God.

It was at this point The Lord began to disassemble the emotional *Jenga* tower I had built one encounter at a time with His Power, Presence, and Love.

CHAPTER 3

WHISPERS AND SHAKINGS

A couple of years after I encountered Holy Spirit in the back pew of that Baptist church, I had to stop by the music store that serviced my daughter's violin. As my car coasted toward a parking space I noticed a man walking across the shopping center parking lot. The sun had just set. There was still brightness in the air, but not enough to illuminate his shadowy figure. As I watched his slow progress from nowhere to nothing, two things happened simultaneously. I became fearful of him, and I had a very strong urge to give him the $20 bill I had in my wallet. In the course of 3-5 seconds I processed through my decision to drive past him, giving in to fear and ignoring the urge to give a stranger money.

The $20 bill haunted me. I did not feel like I could spend it. The pressure inside was really intense and before I spontaneously combusted I decided to sit down with my Bible and prayer to dissect the quick decision I made that evening.

As I considered the event, and asked God to help me get rid of the pressure, I realized that it was not about the man in the parking lot, but what was parking in my heart. I believed the man would be offended if a stranger offered him money. I knew I had no way to know if he would or not, so why did I assume that? Slow realization dawned: I would be offended if a stranger offered me money. But that seemed weird when I said it out loud. Why would I be offended by free money? The first inkling of my pride and self-sufficiency began to dawn in my heart and mind. A small understanding of how these hindered me from drawing near to God began to bloom. It would be a long journey to really open my heart and mind to God, and eventually other people, but the Lord was going to answer my prayer and this was one of the first steps. I searched the Bible to see if this sounded like God and eventually found *1 Kings 19: 11-13 (ESV)*

The Lord said, "Go out and stand on the mountain in the presence of the Lord, for the Lord is about to pass by."

Then a great and powerful wind tore the mountains apart and shattered the rocks before the Lord, but the Lord was not in the wind. After the wind there was an earthquake, but the Lord was not in the earthquake. After the earthquake came a fire, but the Lord was not in the fire. And after the fire came a gentle whisper. When Elijah heard it, he pulled his cloak over his face and went out and stood at the mouth of the cave.

Then a voice said to him, "What are you doing here, Elijah?"

I felt confident that the urge to give the $20 to that man was the Lord's gentle whisper and I resolved to be attentive to His whispers going forward. Eventually, I felt like I could put the $20 in a fundraising fireman's boot, but the lesson shifted something inside of me that began to posture my heart, mind, and soul to listen for the Lord in every moment, interaction and, eventually, adventure.

A year or two later I learned how God also speaks through big shakings. Though my pursuit of Him had resulted in growing by leaps and bounds, I was having trouble giving up some things that I knew He wanted me to give up. Specifically, cigarette smoking.

In 2003 or 2004 I had a series of bouts with bronchitis, then pneumonia. At one fateful visit to my doctor's office, I met with the newest addition to the small practice. He decided to do x-rays of my chest. I knew it would take some time for the results to be ready, but it took a lot longer than expected. I began to worry that he had forgotten me. Finally, he came timidly into the room and sat across from me. He was stumbling on his words, but I managed to piece together that he had every doctor in the office look at the images and they were recommending I go to the emergency room when I left. They could not get an appointment at the radiology center before the following Thursday. If I went to the ER, I could get more detailed imaging sooner. You see, there was a large tumor on my right lung.

I historically stay calm in the midst of crisis. I would only fall apart after everything is finally okay. I was true to form that day.

I thanked him for making the appointment and would consider going to the ER. As I drove home, I just felt drawn to open my heart and mind to the Lord and think things through, rather than rush over to the ER. I don't recall the motions I went through to get home – picking kids up from school, stopping at the grocery store to pick up food to cook for dinner. I know I did them because they were my routine, but the only thing I remember is the idea of imminent death hovering directly between me and every person, action, and thought I had. At that point living life was still a matter of surviving each day. While I knew I would miss my kids if I died, the thought of leaving this world was not all together unpleasant. My only real motivation for living was my son and daughter.

I think I cried and lay in my bed alone for a while talking to God. I don't recall all that I said, or if I railed against Him, I only remember how the conversation ended. I resolved to wait for the appointment the next Thursday, and told God however many days I did or did not have left, every one of them would be lived totally for Him.

The next week I was calm and somewhat resigned to my fate as I waited across the desk for the radiologist to tell me what he saw in the scans.

It took a moment for his words to translate into something I comprehended. "I don't know what they saw, but your lungs are completely clear," he said.

Hot tears sprung to my eyes - an unfortunate side effect of beginning to open my heart to the Lord and life.

Whatever happened, a miraculous removal of a tumor or several doctors misreading an x-ray, the miracle in my heart and mind was real, tangible, and as life altering as that day on the back pew of the Baptist church. I took a deep breath and had a new and different kind of hope I did not quite understand; a hope that I could be a catalyst for change in my own life and other's lives for the glory of God.

CHAPTER 4

TRANSITIONS

In 2006, I began to feel a pressure to leave the small church I had been a part of since 1999. I did not have any sense of going TO anywhere, so I dismissed the small nudges. Over time the nudges grew in strength until I felt like I was losing my mind. I finally made an appointment to meet with one of the associate pastors and his wife for prayer and counsel.

I shared the history of the sense I had to leave our little church, how I had no idea where I was going, and waited for them to tell me what a terrible person I was, and how I needed to pull myself together.

I was shocked when Mark looked across his coffee and said, "If God is calling you out of here then I don't want to see you again on a Sunday morning unless the Lord calls you back. We are about the Kingdom of God, not just our little part of it."

I had no idea how to process ideology that did not serve self- interest first. A perspective of the Kingdom of God that looked to things beyond the immediately visible 'we'. After all the mental and emotional preparation, I expected to be told I should just stay put. Mark's response felt almost like rejection.

In the days following our meeting, I felt openly exposed to the isolation I lived in but plausibly denied to myself through busyness. Without all the activity of serving at my church, I found myself having to face loneliness, bitterness, and many other things I did not want to acknowledge. I did not have the skills to honestly process through my emotions without stuffing, blaming, or engaging in some diversionary activity, so I began to search for a way to fill the space.

Since I did not know what church I was supposed to go to, I decided to start attending my sister's while I waited for the "knowing" that would lead me to my new church home.

I did not grasp that my value was inherent in being created in the image of God, and not in what I did to earn my keep; a concept that would not begin to take hold in my heart and mind until 2014.

For by grace we have been saved through faith. And this is not your own doing; it is the gift of God, not as a result of works, so that no one may boast. Ephesians 2:8-9 (ESV)

Within a few weeks of attending church with my sister, I had found a number of ways to 'plug in,' serve others, and feel like I was worthy of the smiles and hugs I received each week as I walked the halls. I quickly connected to many, but only on a superficial level. I was always busy and able to give, but somehow hide the fact that I was not truly receiving. I believed no one knew my secrets: loneliness and fear that drove a need to control, a lack of belief that the promises of God were actually FOR me, but rather I was to serve and share my story so others would not end up as I had. There was a nagging belief at the edge of my conscious that I had somehow blasphemed Holy Spirit; the only unforgivable sin, and I did not actually have a place waiting for me in heaven.

A year later I was still treading water in this temporary place. I could feel a hunger in me for more, but had heard that it was my own responsibility to "feed myself" spiritually if I was not leaving satisfied on Sundays. I read my Bible daily, delving deep into the study notes, read book after book on church history, how to be a better wife, mother, and volunteer. While these all stirred my affections for the Lord and grew me as a woman of God, the deep craving inside was simply not getting satisfied.

In early 2007, one of the Sunday services was a replay of a visiting pastor named Mark Driscoll. I only recall that I left that video teaching with a fire ignited in me I had not felt before. I could feel a tap into the deeper things of God that had been briefly touched during the 30-minute sermon and was compelled to find out how to get more of it.

My research turned up that Mark was the lead pastor of a church in Seattle, Washington. It is clear in scripture that we are to be in close community as a part of our walk as believers, and though I had never been successful in lowering my internal walls enough to genuinely let others in, I prioritized the ability to be with people in person. In the midst of considering moving to Washington state, I came across a link for Acts 29, a church planting network. There were two associated churches in DFW – one in Keller and one in Highland Village. Both more than a 30 minute drive from my home. With the firm belief God would not want me attending church so far away, I dissuaded myself from making the trek to either one.

But God.

Proverbs 16:9 (ESV) says "The heart of a man plans his way, but the Lord establishes his steps."

For years I thought this meant that God would take me wherever He wanted me to go regardless of what I wanted or planned. In 2015, I did some study of the original language and the various ways those words can be understood. What I found was quite a paradigm shift. The verse seemed to be about how we imagine our plans and future and God establishes the path to get us there. However, He is not a genie in a bottle. He does not give snakes, even when we ask for them thinking we are asking for bread. But when we are asking for bread and don't know how to receive it? He teaches us how to eat.

He knew I was hungry for the deeper things of Him. He knew the freedom and fullness of life I imagined in the buried and hidden parts of my heart. He began to make a way for me to get there.

He started gently. I would hear about the Acts29 church in Highland Village a lot. Sometime multiple times in a week. I started to think about visiting my sister on a Sunday. She lived in the same town and I could easily stop by the church after a visit to her. However, our schedules never seemed to work out.

Eventually, every which way I turned, I would hear the name "The Village Church" or "Matt Chandler." I was getting irritated and actually thought the enemy was coming against me at one point. I could not tell you why, but I absolutely KNEW that God would not want me to drive 30 minutes to attend church.

I don't know what day of the week it was when the email came in with an audio file from a recent teaching by Matt Chandler. He was teaching through Luke, but I do not remember a single word of his sermon. What is burned into my heart and mind as vividly today, nine years later, is the end of the sermon. Pastor Matt dismissed everyone with "I love you guys more than you know."

I felt the truth of his words in my bones. It did not make any sense how someone that did not even know I existed could possibly love me, but I had no doubt that he did. And after serving under Pastor Matt for eight years, I know his love for God and God's people is deep and genuine. That genuine love is what finally provoked me to make the 30 minute trek that very next Sunday.

As I walked into the sanctuary and found a seat in the back of the room, I felt peace and a sense of coming home. I had arrived early, which is on-time to me, and spent time reflecting on the journey that brought me there that day. It was clear the Lord had shepherded me to this place. Now I just needed to figure out why.

.

CHAPTER 5

PERSPECTIVE

I walked into the sanctuary with worn carpet and sat on the far left side of the room about seven or eight rows back. My first sensation was of having come home. Peacefulness flooded me. I exhaled deeply and realized I had been holding my breath. As I sat in the seat waiting for service to begin, I became very aware of my aloneness and the weight of isolation around me. I felt like a 'them' in a room full of 'us'. At the time, I thought not belonging was about the people in the room not noticing me, but would eventually learn it was really about what was going on in my own heart and mind. I was beginning to recognize the weight of the emotional walls I had built attempting to protect myself from the harsh and uncaring world around me.

Eventually someone came to the front to greet the room and kick off the festivities of Sunday service. The music was good and I felt it hook into my heart, but it scared me that people around me were raising their hands while they sang and swayed with the worship flooding the room. During the second song my fear of "the crazies" around me was overpowered by my fear of becoming a crazy myself. I was beginning to feel a pressing urge to raise *my* hands! I did not pay much attention to the teaching that week. I was too preoccupied with trying to process, dissect and control what was going on inside of me.

I left as soon as the teaching was over, but began to attend as often as my schedule would allow. It was not long before I knew this was the place I had been moving toward since the faint stirrings to leave my small church in 2006.

Each week I fought the desire to raise my hands during worship; my mind just could not let go of the idea that I would become something to be rejected by normal Christians if I was not perfectly still and quiet in God's house.

As time went on, and I continued to arrive ridiculously early, I started opening the Bible stored under the seats to pass the time and take my mind off the wrestling in my spirit that would come with worship. But God. He has such a great sense of humor. Several weeks in a row, regardless of where I sat, the Bible opened to *Nehemiah 8:6 (ESV)*

And Ezra blessed the LORD*, the great God, and all the people answered, "Amen, Amen," lifting up their hands. And they bowed their heads and worshiped the* LORD *with their faces to the ground.*

The second time one of the Bibles randomly opened to the verse, I thought "That's weird."

The fifth time I opened to *Nehemiah 8:6*, sitting in a different seat, opening a different Bible, a holy fear filled me.

A consuming realization came over me. God was actually *talking to me* and HE WANTED ME TO BE A CRAZY! HE WANTED ME TO RAISE MY HANDS IN CHURCH!

I was not able to understand then that God was actually communicating an invitation to me. He was inviting me to demonstrate my love for Him in a way that would open me to receive His love in deeper ways for myself.

It took weeks of wrestling with my pride until I was finally willing to look "foolish" for the Lord. The consistent reminder that the folks in the Bible lifted their hands to the Lord in praise finally wore me down. I committed to at least TRY lifting my hands while singing during Sunday service.

I don't know what date it finally happened. I do recall the room around me. Bodies standing in a sea of color. My heart pounding a million miles an hour. Would anyone be looking at me? Would anyone laugh at me? What if I caused someone else to stumble by distracting them from the Lord during worship? As the first song began I felt awkward; like *everyone* in the room was aware of my struggle. I would begin to raise one hand, the other clinched tightly, and then the first would drop back to my side. The mental battle was on – would I choose fear or my Father in heaven? The thoughts jockeying back and forth were making me emotionally and spiritually nauseous.

It would be great if I won the battle that day, but I did not. I kept arriving early, sitting in different seats, and the Bible kept opening up to verses about lifting hands to the Lord. I was both thankful and perturbed that there were so many passages mentioning this act of humble acknowledgment of our Creator. The mental battle raged each week as the music played, until finally, one day, both hands just shot up in the air.

Full of surprise and wonder, I felt a bit heady. I worshipped the Lord wholeheartedly, but it felt like a song of victory, not love and adoration. Immediately I began to criticize myself, and compare my experience to other people's 'free worship.'

It felt like I jumped out of the frying pan and into the fryer. Victory in one area exposed another area my thoughts and opinions had been raised against the truth of who God is and who He says I am in Him.

Initially I was discouraged and wondered if I should even continue to lift my hands when I felt led to, but then I was led to the *2 Corinthians 3:16-18 (ESV)*

"But when one turns to the Lord, the veil is removed. Now the Lord is the Spirit, and where the Spirit of the Lord is, there is freedom. And we all, with unveiled face, beholding the glory of the Lord, are being transformed into the same image from one degree of glory to another. For this comes from the Lord who is the Spirit."

I had confidence I had turned to the Lord; therefore, the veil must be removed. I was encouraged but also perplexed. I really did not know *what veil* had been removed.

I am inquisitive and my mind can race down rabbit trails at quite a rapid rate. It can trigger anxiety if I don't stop myself and write my questions down so I can seek answers when my mind has slowed down again, so I began journaling.

The Lord is the Spirit, and where He is there is freedom. That meant I could be free. But free to do what? Or free to NOT DO what?

The veil is gone, and I get to behold the glory of the Lord which transforms me into His image one degree of glory at a time. How is a degree of glory measured? How fast can you be transformed into a degree of glory? How many degrees are there?

I was starting to get it. This would be a journey, not a destination I arrived at when I received salvation.

Some years later I would be walking to my car after work and be captivated by the visual parable unfolding before my eyes. Perspective changes. We can see little from some perspectives and much from others. But only God can see all perspectives at all times.

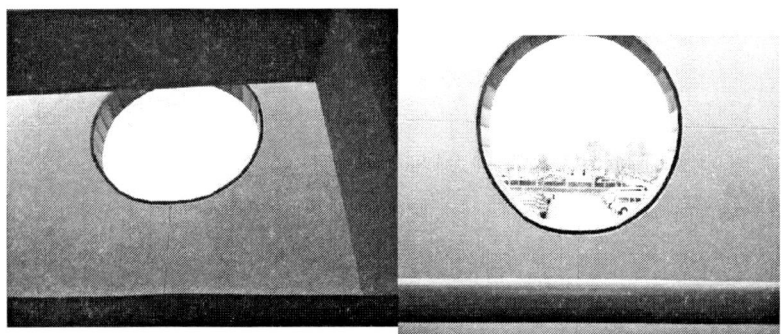

Bottom of the stairwell   Half-way up the stairwell

View from the top of the parking garage

Now faith is the assurance of things hoped for, the conviction of things not seen. For by it, the people of old received their commendation. By faith we understand that the universe was created by the word of God, so that what is seen was not made out of things that are visible…By faith Abraham obeyed when he was called to go out to a place that he was to receive as an inheritance. And he went out, not knowing where he was going. By faith he went to live in the land of promise, as in a foreign land, living in tents with Isaac and Jacob, heirs with him of the same promise. For he was looking forward to the city that has foundations, whose designer and builder is God.

Therefore, since we are surrounded by so great a cloud of witnesses, let us also lay aside every weight, and sin which clings so closely, and let us run with endurance the race that is set before us, looking to Jesus, the founder and perfecter of our faith, who for the joy that was set before him endured the cross, despising the shame, and is seated at the right hand of the throne of God. Consider him who endured from sinners such hostility against himself, so that you may not grow weary or fainthearted.

Hebrews 11:1-3,8-10   Hebrews 12:1-3 (ESV)

CHAPTER 6

FAITH WALK

My understanding of God and the power of prayer grew. My faith did too, in one way. But personally walking by faith became difficult for me as I began to see more and more of my prophetic prayers for others become reality. On the one hand my faith grew deeply for what the Lord was willing to do for others. On the other, cynicism began to creep into my heart regarding what I believed God would do for me.

I had a knack for knowing when babies were coming. On my birthday one year I felt led to pray for one of my pastors and his wife to get pregnant and have a little girl. They already had two sons, so it seemed like a stretch prayer to me at the time. Until a few months later when I found out they were pregnant and the baby's due date was exactly one year to the day from my prayer! Holy Spirit prompted me to buy them a little dress as a prophetic act (something I do in the natural to declare my faith God will do what He promised He would). Guess what? They had a little girl.

One December I shared with my home group leaders that Holy Spirit had told me one of the women in our group would get pregnant in February. She and her husband had been trying for many years to get pregnant, so I did not tell her, but wanted to have partners in praying for this to come to pass. Again, she did get pregnant in February and now has a beautiful daughter!

These two examples were both times of rejoicing and of jealousy. Answered prayers for others pressed on places in my heart that I was bitter toward the Lord. Particularly, where I believed God was ignoring my petitions for my children and myself. I wanted the Lord to fix all the consequences in our lives that stemmed from my brokenness when they were younger. I also wanted to feel like I belonged and be a part of community. It felt like people only loved me because of the gifts the Lord poured out through me. On an intellectual level I knew this was not true, but the familiar lies that would come to my mind plagued me with despair of ever partaking of the life I saw others living each day. This despair created filters I viewed everything through. Though my life was on a very clear trajectory of restoration, I was not able to see many of the answered prayers for what they were. I continued to feel like I was on the outside looking in.

Interestingly, over the years I mentored women in the Recovery/Steps ministry, I found myself hearing this same thread of despair in their stories. Neither I, nor the ladies I met with, would dare to speak it out loud, but we clearly believed the Lord would not do good things for *us*.

As I processed my own misunderstanding realization began to dawn that I was clinging to unbelief in the face of many good things the Lord did for me on a daily basis, and even in the face of powerful miracles I experienced.

In January 2013 a notice came out that my church was going to Israel. I didn't think much of the trip until my friend Clarissa felt the Lord press on her that He wanted me to go on the trip. I trusted her when it came to what the Lord shared with her, so I could not dismiss the idea even though the cost without a roommate was over $5000.

I lived pay check to pay check at the time. As I prayed and considered the ten day trip I went through my budget for the month. After I cut a little from groceries, gas, and some other small things I came up with $40. I withdrew the money from the ATM and stuck it in an envelope I had decorated. After saying to God, "That's what I have to put toward the trip to Israel. If you want me to go, you have to provide the rest of the money" I put the envelope above my fireplace.

The colorful "ISRAEL" envelope sat on my fireplace mantle as a daily reminder to pray. I spent the next few weeks sharing the story with a real negative bend. My message was one of doubt that I would be on the trip that summer. 'I know the Lord is able but…"

February 10, 2013 I went to a nearby charismatic church. I always encountered Him in powerful ways when I was there, and that day was no exception. As I raised my hands and eyes to heaven I heard the Lord *audibly* say, "I am sending you to Israel". The voice was firm and powerful and full of love while not leaving any room to argue. Everything in my mind soul and spirit simply *submitted*. I immediately *believed* I was going, though I had no idea how that would happen.

As I shared the story of my *repentance* and new belief the Lord would make the way for me to go to Israel I was surprised to find how many people wanted to participate in this adventure with the Lord. Many people gave financially and prayed for provision as well. Still, just before the final due date I needed a significant amount of money. I went for a walk at work one afternoon and confessed my tiny doubt that the Lord would come through on this. As I returned to my desk my manager called me into a side office. I received news that the bonus program at work would actually pay out the day the final payment was due and the amount I received was more than I needed. In only 33 days, I was able mail my check by the final due date and secure a spot on the trip to Israel.

One of the things I think is common for all of us is that our work for the Lord is not very public. Faithfulness to serve is seen only by the angels and God. Often, the Lord speaks to me in the strange details of day-to-day life and I simply trust He is doing good things through me because He is not wasteful or manipulative. I have recorded thousands of voice memos and filled close to 50 journals since 2012 and often only recognize the fruit of my labors for the Lord years later when I review these. But I see enough fruit from the seeds of faith I have sown to believe *1 Corinthians 15:58 (ESV)*

Therefore, my beloved brothers, be steadfast, immovable, always abounding in the work of the Lord, knowing that in the Lord your labor is not in vain.

The trip to Israel finally arrived and was an adventure from the start.

For instance, upon arrival to Israel I was separated from my group and taken aside by the Israeli security for questioning. It always interests me how these moments are never scary to me as they unfold, but only later as I think back on how they *might have gone*.

Half way through the trip, on our last night in Tiberius, I walked into town with a couple of the girls to look for cheap bathing suits. We would be at the Dead Sea the next day. Two warnings for the ladies were:

- do not shave for at least one day prior. The extremely high mineral content can cause pain in even the slightest skin irritation.
- the mud can stain clothes.

After an unsuccessful search, we headed back toward the hotel so we could prepare for departure the next morning. As we walked along the Sea of Galilee I felt a sudden, sharp pain in my right heel. I stopped and pulled my foot up to see what had happened. Shock from the pain combined with genuine disbelief at what I found took a moment to clear. A screw had gone through the bottom of my flip-flop and deep enough into my foot to attach the shoe to my body. After a few deep breaths to get control of the pain and decide what I needed to do next I noticed a place to sit about 20 feet away. I began to hobble toward it. As I did, the natural pull on my sandal ripped the screw out of my foot. It did not bleed as badly as some areas would have, but blood still pooled and sloshed as I hobbled back to the hotel with the help of my friends.

There was not much commotion from the staff as we approached the front desk. Without much ado, they offered me iodine and a couple of small bandages so I could deal with the wound myself. There was a small bit of me that was disappointed by the lack of drama and I murmured to myself as I went to my room.

I let my foot bleed for several minutes under running water in the bathtub before I began to apply pressure to stop the bleeding. I used the small bandages to cover up the deep hole in my foot, and hoped they would absorb the blood.

Self-pity began to speak to me as I made my way slowly downstairs to the rest of the group laughing and planning for the next day. As pain shot through my body with the slightest pressure on my foot, I recalled a mesquite thorn going into my heel when I was young. I could not walk on it for days. Walking was a large part of experiencing Israel. I heaved a big sigh as I resigned myself to missing out on the activities of the next day and maybe beyond.

News travels fast and after the team expressed their concerns and sympathy they prayed for healing. I said a dutiful amen and when we were done socializing for the evening I went to bed mopey.

I woke the next morning, walked to the bathroom and began to brush my teeth. It took a few moments before I remembered I should not be able to stand at the sink with my weight on my right foot. I tapped my heel to see if my foot was numb for some reason. I felt the thump, but no pain.

I flipped my foot over and saw a black dot in the place that the screw had gone in but there was no pain. No broken skin. No scab.

I went down stairs and shared the news as we gathered to load onto the bus. The general reaction was similar to mine. Surprise and mild disbelief.

We hiked a steep hill that day, and I kept up.

We floated in the Dead Sea and I felt no pain.

At the sea, when I took off my flip-flop to test the waters, I braced myself for the searing pain of salt in a wound, but none came.

I was walking in a miracle and with every step I took that day, I expected pain to shoot up my leg.

It wasn't until a few years later when I was sharing the story that it struck me. That is how I respond to most of the amazing things the Lord does in me, through me, and for me.

I anticipate His taking back the good gift that He gives.

I asked God to heal this strong-hold. To reach in to the wounds from life that had hardened into the unbelief that had such a firm hold on my heart and mind. I asked God to help me walk in *full* belief of His goodness.

CHAPTER 7

BECOMING BEAUTIFUL

One word I longed to hear directed toward me my whole life, but did not, is "beautiful."

If you look at photos of me through my life you may be surprised by this. I was very beautiful physically, but was full of self-hatred, bound by shame and immersed in my world-view of being a victim. I could not receive anything other than the barbed words that matched my own internal dialogue.

For most of my life I only ate one meal every day, usually a small bowl of cereal. Then I went through a season of exactly measuring my food intake and exercise caloric burn. My life revolved around trying to garner the smallest bit of affirmation from my husband, but the only attention overt enough for me to recognize came from other men. At some point I decided that being physically attractive was the root of all my problems and over the course of a few years, gained over 100 pounds.

One of the first things that I learned as my waist began to bulge was that I had no value for myself if I was not turning the heads of men. Their attention, however inappropriate, was a source of validating my existence and purpose. As the years passed, I realized that I had no ability to view myself as lovable, valuable, or worthy of anything good because my body was "gross." I began an internal struggle trying to change my external appearance.

I would lose a few pounds, then gain more back. My size bounced up and down as the battle waxed and waned in my mind and soul.

I hated my body, but I hated being noticed by men more. My marriage was in shambles and with all the twisted thoughts and beliefs I had brought with me from my past, the attention of men provoked a twisted internal cycle of shame, guilt, loneliness, and anger. I would spend hours reading my Bible trying to force myself to believe what God says about me as one of His own.

Thankfully, The Lord is with us in the battles, and He is with us in the war.

I hated my body when I had a 24-inch waist. I hated my body when I had curves and people told me I looked like Marilyn Monroe, and I hated my body when I was eating well, exercising, and making progress towards my health goal. Slowly a realization emerged, I didn't hate my body, I hated myself.

It is odd to me how I could not articulate the truth of the matter. I could not knowingly state I hated myself when I knew, intellectually at least, that God loved me. That God formed me and made me for His plans and purposes. I could not hate what God loved, so I hated what I thought He must hate as well- all my sin which was padding my body. I had no concept of what His grace really meant to me, individually, in the 'now'. I could barely believe that someday in eternity it would be "a better place."

Then, in March 2012, I went on a mission trip to South Sudan. During the weeks leading up to the trip several people came to me and shared that they felt impressed this would be a special time for me and the Lord.

Spending 10 days with people you do not know very well can be a challenging experience, but I was blessed to be with an amazing group of people. I felt particularly connected with a woman named Erin. One of the early emerging patterns on this trip was that she and I would separately spend time with the Lord, and when the group came back together, we had both been led to the same verses in scripture to meditate upon and study! Because she was such an amazing and godly woman, it grew my confidence that I not only heard, but could distinguish, the Lord's voice.

As the week progressed I felt the nearness of the Lord more tangibly. We helped plant a new church in the border town of Kaya which sits at a dusty crossroads between Uganda, South Sudan, and the Congo. The power of God was manifest and many people gave their lives to the Lord in just a few days.

On one of the three hour treks between Yei and Kaya I found myself slipping into one of those sweet in-between states of consciousness as the rhythm of the rutted road rocked me in the back of the vehicle. I pictured myself on the ground next to Jesus sitting in heaven on his throne. The holes in his feet and hands were highlighted by the light of radiant glory shining through them. I saw my heart muscle sitting in my hand that rested on His knee, exposed outside my chest, ready to receive from Him. These imaginations helped me to be genuinely vulnerable with

God. I listened with my whole self and jumped when I heard, "I am making you beautiful in my sight."

My heart raced. What did that even mean? I grabbed my Bible and looked up "beautiful" in the concordance.

There is a gate in the wall of Jerusalem called Beautiful.

Proverbs 31 (ESV) says *charm is deceitful and beauty is vain but a woman who fears the Lord is to be praised.* Okay, this was helpful. I asked the Lord to give me that sort of fear of Him. Clearly it did not involve cowering, or it would not garner praise.

Then I read *1 Peter.* The entire book was a timely encouragement but in chapter 3 verse 4 (ESV), it says, *"but let your adorning be the hidden person of the heart with the imperishable beauty of a gentle and quiet spirit, which in God's sight is very precious".*

A gentle and quiet spirit. This is *precious* in God's sight. Condemnation tried to creep in and tell me I was not qualified. I did not have a gentle or quiet spirit. I could feel bitterness and offense rising up in me.

After all I have been through, how could I possibly be gentle or quiet!? That's not fair, I thought.

Immediately, a verse in Philippians popped into my head and I began to understand I did not have to BE anything *because* of what I had been through. I am *able* to be gentle and meek through Jesus' strength.

"Not that I am speaking of being in need, for I have learned in whatever situation I am to be content. I know how to be brought low, and I know how to abound. In any and every circumstance, I have learned the secret of facing plenty and hunger, abundance and need. I

can do all things through him who strengthens me." Philippians 4:11-13 (ESV)

As I bounced around the back of the Land Rover, I gave God permission to make me beautiful in His sight - whatever that meant. I asked Him for a gentle and quiet spirit. Thinking back to the verse I had just read, I said, "You can bring me low, you can make me abound. I *choose* to be content as you do this work in me."

At the end of the two weeks, I returned to the US. He indeed began the work of chiseling, comforting, teaching, growing, and humbling as He had promised to do. I did not even see the intricate details until almost four years later, as I went through several old journals from various months and years. My breath was taken away as I began to see a pattern emerge that connected the dots of God's encounters and works in my life across that span of time.

Soon after I returned from Sudan I began to be bombarded by people telling me how beautiful I was. The strangest instance being a teen girl skipping up to my car and sticking her head through my rolled down window. It startled the heck out of me when she yelled, "YOU ARE SO BEAUTIFUL!" It also freaked me out a little bit. A word I had longed to hear for my whole life was suddenly being lobbed at me from many unexpected directions. Often I would not have makeup on, or would be leaving the gym sweaty and hair frazzled and frizzing in a puffy halo around my head.

I felt a pressure building inside. Something was going to have to give, and I wanted it to be my misunderstandings and not God's truth. In many of these moments I had to stop myself and read scripture out-loud. It was my attempt to let my heart and mind rest in God and purposely reset and refresh my spirit in the Word of God. It was not always easy to make this choice. Contentment was often hard to find. Sometimes I would *angrily* shout at heaven, "I CHOOSE TO BE CONTENT AS YOU DO THIS WORK!"

In June 2012 I heard of a prayer house in Dallas that had prophecy rooms – a place where people would pray and seek the Lord's heart to encourage the body of Christ. I was skeptical of allowing a perfect stranger to supposedly tell me what God had to say to me. I had only experienced this sort of encouragement from close friends and it was done in very cautious language. I also had some fear that the people gifted this way would somehow be able to know things that would be embarrassing to me, like how angry and violent I had once been. What if they told me I am not really saved? But one of my dearest friends was going to receive a prophetic word and I agreed to go with her one weekend. Or maybe she agreed to go with me. The Lord was stirring my curiosity by this time, and His gentle ways are always so patient. I often find I end up in the right place at the right time simply because God is bigger than the box I try to put Him in.

So, we signed up. Though it was uncommon, we went in to the prayer room together. I was so relieved when they explained they would pray and listen for the Lord's heart for us today, what He wants to say to us and about us and that it would be done in love and for the purpose of building up and encouraging *(1 Corinthians 13 and 14).*

The encounter was very encouraging, though a bit odd. I had distinct impressions from the Lord showing me which prophetic words were His, and which came from the people mustering something from their own strength. I later learned this was "discernment."

I had forgotten about this prophecy until spring 2016, when I felt an urge to scroll through my phone's voice memos. I did not know why I was looking through them, but I always follow what I believe are God's promptings if at all possible. "Natalie and Michelle's word" caught my eye, and I listened. They prophesied to my friend first and I was encouraged to realize how much had come to pass for her! Then I heard my name.

One of the men began to share the vision he was seeing. He saw Father God taking me from room to room to room. Each room was painted a different vibrant color, and was brightly lit. Inside each room was a different man who apologized for some way that God the Father, Son, and Holy Spirit had been misrepresented to me throughout my life. In each room, the Lord took a piece of my heart from the man within and placed it back inside of me. God was restoring all the parts of my heart. And when He was done, there would not even be lines where the pieces were put back together. By my response on the recording, I clearly did not understand the prophecy given to me that day.

As the recorded voices continued, the Lord brought to my remembrance a sunny morning in 2013. I had arrived late to work. As I drove past the garage sign I saw there were only 19 of about 2000 parking spaces open. Not wanting to waste time hunting for the impossible, I determined to park somewhere on the street. As I rounded the curve of the street toward the garage entrance the Lord gave me a powerful image of a specific parking space on the 4th floor. I submitted to entering the garage with a bad attitude, and I lobbed a sarcastic prayer toward God. "Fine, I will drive to the fourth floor before parking on the street. But don't let me be late to my meeting."

As I circled the concrete center path up each level of the garage, I passed several open spots. I kept asking the Lord, "Can I park *here?*" and He would say "No, I have made a place for you. Keep going"

So I kept going. And going. And going. I seriously thought I had passed all 19 spots on the short drive to the top floor. But, as I rounded the corner on the fourth floor and saw the sea of cars before me, I was humbled and repentant. I saw the exact place the Lord had shown me, open and waiting for me to park in it. It reminded me of when Jesus promises that He is going to make a place for us in His father's house. I wanted to understand what it means to have a place prepared for me by the Lord. I instinctively understood awareness of my unique design was a key component in the work of becoming beautiful in God's sight.

As the memory of parking in the prepared place rolled through my mind, the Lord transitioned the image to Father's Day 2015. Our pastor had felt Holy Spirit was prompting us to set aside the teaching plan for the morning so we could pray and prophesy over one another. There were five people in my group and we took turns speaking life giving words to one another. One of the men sitting with my group had a very vivid picture as he prayed for me. He saw me sitting in a fire watching doors go past. As I sat, the fire seared things off of me that needed to be broken off. He heard the Father say He was pleased with me. I had been patient in the waiting and it was time to run. The right door was about to open.

It took time, prayer and reviewing journals, but I was finally able to see the connection between the three prophetic words and how they had impacted me.

With the first prophetic word, the Lord revealed the healing work He was going to do over the next few years, 2012 through 2016. Only looking back at all that had happened since the prophecy was shared with me could I see how it applied to my life. Many visions, dreams, and encouragements that I had not been able to interpret or apply at the time they occurred received clarity through the process of looking back. The events the Lord used to heal my heart often felt like hell on earth as I went through them. But God made them full of life as they led me through the process of becoming who I was made to be. It was a journey through healing and learning to live in a place of hope and abundance no matter the circumstances in my life.

With the second prophetic word, the Lord was giving me encouragement to persevere in the midst of the process. He was giving me the firm confidence that He has a plan and will not let me stop too early. I could trust He would carry me to the very place He had prepared for me and I only need to be attentive to His voice and follow Him rather than my own assessment of good places to stop along the road.

Finally, the third prophetic word let me know the process the Lord began in 2012 was near completion, three years later. Through the prophetic words of my friend, God reminded me the refining fire is for my good and recognized my faithfulness to sit in that place. The vision also acknowledged the many times I had *not gone through doors* and continued waiting on the Lord. My friend had no idea about any of the circumstances in my life or previous encounters with the Lord. Knowing their ignorance made their words more than simple encouragement. They renewed my faith and hope in God in a way that I had not realized that I needed. I was refreshed in my spirit to continue to wait on the Lord and run hard after the things that bless Him and the people I encounter each day. This is just how prophecy should work!

I began to see all of the pieces and parts of my life over the last four years come together to form a tapestry the Lord had been weaving all along.

While I had not always seen results for all the people, all the places, all of the miles of driving while praying and worshipping the Lord just because He asked me to do these things, I had trusted in the truth of *1 Corinthians 15:58 (ESV)*

"Therefore, my beloved brothers, be steadfast, immovable, always abounding in the work of the Lord, knowing that in the Lord your labor is not in vain."

Every single moment of waiting was cleansing my inner wounds, purifying my concepts of who God is, and preparing me for the work the Lord has for me. I realized every word He spoke that had seemingly not come to fruition was still germinating! "Life" had been (and still is) a process working to prepare the soil of my heart to receive the seeds of faith the Lord had sown. It broke down the shell of the seed, and brought deep nourishment to the identity the Lord knit into me. It would be almost one year later, in spring 2016, that a friend of mine would walk up to me and say, "I just saw a picture of the first sprout of a seed germinating above you. A little green shoot with a leaf ready to unfold." They had no idea what a powerful image that was for me!

"The Lord is not slow to fulfill his promise as some count slowness, but is patient toward you, not wishing that any should perish, but that all should reach repentance" 2 Peter 3:9 (ESV)

What seems like delay is Him bringing us to a full change of heart; to see as He sees, and want as He wants.

This healing of my heart culminated in early 2016 with a transformation of how I view love.

I had a deep understanding of covenant love. Love that laid down its life for another. Love that considered another person's need over its own.

In the first month of 2016 I sat in a meeting at work where someone passed me a stick of gum. The shiny wrapper had truth or dare questions all over it. I had not seen this before and posted a picture on social media. Someone asked, "which one spoke to you?"

I honestly had not read them, so I looked at the picture.

One of the phrases said: "Do you believe in love at first sight?"

I laughed out loud. "Of course not," I mumbled to myself. "That's just hormones."

The Lord's gentle voice washed over me.

"You don't even believe in being in love," He said.

I felt a hard knot in my chest and tingling over my body, which is what happens when I realize I've missed something really important and don't know how I did, like picking my kids up from school or paying the mortgage.

I sort of held my breath and thought about it for a minute.

God was right. I did not believe people when they would post pictures of their babies with captions like "So in love!"

I was highly skeptical of people who would say awesome things about their spouse of 20 years and giggle together.

"Being in love isn't real," I said to the heavens above.

"Yes it is." was God's simple reply. After a pause, He said, "It is why you were the JOY set before me on the cross."

Oh boy. I had not had much joy in the love I had given. I did not give it begrudgingly, but it was my duty, my *proof* that I loved others. But joy? I couldn't say there was much of that. It was my pleasure to love my family and those the Lord brought into my life. Something I was glad to do for the fruit it produced.

The concept of a different sort of love sank a bit deeper into me and something inside my heart cracked open, and the light of God shone into a new place.

I remembered my son being born and marveling at his tiny fingers and toes, love flooding me to the point of tears.

And my daughter, who didn't cry out for a few minutes after she was born. I recalled the nurses rushed around her while I lay helpless on the hospital bed, wondering what was going on, and then the relief that flooded me when I finally heard her crackly fresh-born cries.

Tears streamed down my face sitting at my desk in the middle of my office. I realized I could not even read the words on my computer screen, but I didn't care.

What a very big and amazing God we get to be in relationship with, that can use a silly gum wrapper to bring such a deep healing to a woman whose heart had been crushed and without hope for most of her life.

This is the sort of love I had been longing for. I could sense this was going to be a catalyst to see a much longed for restoration and reconciliation between me and my children, sister, mom, and other family.

When I look back and remember I am always struck by my impatience. How, in the moment I pray, I really expect the Lord to respond instantly – a puff of smoke, that I would blink my eyes and everything be different. That it would be all better, the way *I have asked Him to make it.*

I would get frustrated day after day watching my prayers for others be answered in amazing ways, while my own requests appeared to be hindered at every hint of coming forth. But there was always a moment when I got a fresh glimpse of my life. I would see the distance between "back then" and "right now" And realize the goodness in the Lord's ways over my own. Looking back I could see how the path unfolded differently than I asked, and it was a much better way.

God sees. He knows. He is always giving us His very best and leading us to more of His best.

It occurred to me that I was not actually *becoming* beautiful in God's sight. I was beginning to *believe* the words of Jesus on the cross, "It is finished." I have been beautiful in God's sight from before the foundations of the earth, when He planned how He would form me in my mother's womb, how He would woo me to faith in Him, and how He would love me into looking more and more like Jesus each day.

The most transformative aspect of this season was getting to a place in my heart that I could begin to genuinely trust

God. He is working out my good in all things, every moment, even when I am not able to see His goodness in the circumstance in front of me.

CHAPTER 8

ABIDING

Journeys transform us. We cannot undo the change brought by seeing the things we saw, feeling the things we felt. We can never go back to who we were, even if we long for those places like the Israelites longed for Egypt.

From the moment I felt the Holy Spirit rush through me in 1999 my heart cry was to bring glory to God. He saw that passion through the hot mess that I was. When He encountered me in that back pew, I drank daily, smoked cigarettes, cursed like a sailor, had anger and bitterness so deeply buried I was blind to it until just after an angry outburst occurred, usually directed toward my son. Then guilt and shame would consume me until it had festered into another outburst of anger.

I had come a long way from being that angry bitter woman when I boarded my first flight to Sudan in July 2010. I was full of peace and joy by the time I went on my second trip in March 2012 and the Lord began the deep work of showing me how beautiful I am in His sight. (Well, really, how beautiful WE are in His sight.)

Along the way, He has given me intense encounters with His presence, and powerful visual images to illustrate His truth.

As one of the consequences of my past, I had a very hard time receiving from others. Before God could open me up to receive from others, He had to bring me to a place I could really receive from *Him*. And not with an attitude of feeling like some taskmaster had finally, grudgingly, given to the groveling smelly servant.

No, He wanted me to receive as a *beloved member of His family*.

He created us in His image, and part of His image is community in the Trinity. Community requires being vulnerable and exposed. I wasn't really interested in this, but God is faithful to answer our prayers even when we don't understand what we asked for. I had asked for full inner healing and He was answering my request with a YES! Sometimes He heals in an instant, and other times, it is a very long journey with Him.

One day the word 'abide' caught my attention. I don't recall how it did, but it rolled around in my head until I couldn't take it anymore. I have a process, though the order of actions vary. When a word, phrase or concept catches in my head I search the Bible for it. Then I look up the meaning in a dictionary, thesaurus, encyclopedia, and use the internet to search for other bits of information. I have a natural knack for tracking and comparing information to quickly sort through what is accurate and what is junk. Then I focus on the information that seems to be good to dig into further. Eventually I figured out this process needed to begin by asking Holy Spirit to lead me, and then listen to those 'gut checks' that He gives.

In researching the word 'abide,' I started with the definition on Dictionary.com.

1. to remain; continue; stay:
2. to have one's abode; dwell; reside:
3. to continue in a particular condition, attitude, relationship, etc.; last.

I then looked up all the instances the word occurred in the Bible, and decided to focus on the 29 occurrences in the ESV new testament. All but two are part of writings by the apostle John, and in some way relay the image of abiding in Jesus being necessary as a follower of His; to be able to ask God for things and receive them.

I researched and studied many aspects of this idea, including how the early Israelites might understand the concept. My head was spinning.

Rest, doing things 'in His name', producing fruit, being a branch. After hours and hours of reading, highlighting, and feeling like I had more questions than answers, I *finally* cried out, "What the heck does this mean?!"

I put the study of abiding back on my 'shelf.' A place I put the mysterious, the frustrating, the things I am worn out trying to understand or am too weirded out to even go near at the moment.

I love when God takes things off that shelf. Late 2013, as I stood worshipping during a Thursday night prayer meeting, the Lord used my imagination to show me an image of Jesus standing in front of me. Looking right at me. I looked back and my heart was full of love and adoration. I sang to Him with everything in me. Then I saw him turn His back to me, take a step backward, and occupy the same space I was standing in.

I could see both of our bodies when I looked down- they were slightly transparent. I saw our two hearts begin to merge into one another. Then I saw my blood vessels and Jesus blood vessels connected to the one heart and the blood pumping through both of our bodies was the same blood. Our chests rose and fell at the same rate with each breath we inhaled and exhaled. I felt something in me relinquish control of my life to Jesus. My trust in Him and belief that He is *for* me and not *against* me took a deeper hold in my mind and heart.

When the song was finished I sat down and began to journal about my experience. One of the interns at the prayer house called out to me before the service began. Across the room she announced while pointing at me, "Lady with the long curly hair - yeah, it was sort of weird. During one of the worship songs I saw God's heart and your heart merge into one heart!"

Tears sprung to my eyes. The sense of God's love overpowered me, and I could barely catch my breath.

Someone I had never met, didn't know who I was or anything about me, had SEEN part of the SAME picture Holy Spirit had shown me! I felt affirmed in my being His child, being connected to Him, and that I am able to abide in Him. The immediate desire that sprung up in me was to abide more.

In just a few moments I had the beginning of real understanding of abiding that hours and hours of research had not been able to produce.

I recalled a verse that said something about Holy Spirit being our teacher and made a note in my journal so I could be sure to start researching that topic soon.

I love the written word of God. I love to study it, and I continue to this day to dig in to the history, context, and original language meaning as I study scripture each day. I find great joy, pleasure, and understanding of our good Father in these things. But His personal lessons, tailored to how He knit me together to interact and experience Him, consistently give me the deepest understanding of His love, nature, and character.

There are so many layers to the Lord's purposes in each of our lives. In every moment, every action He is working in a thousand unseen ways, but I see a primary purpose is the work of conforming us into the image of Jesus. While primarily shaping and molding me, these encounters have also been really valuable in the heat of hard circumstances.

I purposely leave out many of the details of my life because I want to show honor to those that have been a part of it. Know that my daughter gave me permission to share this part of our story.

In July 2014, I received a text that she was being taken to the emergency room. During the next weeks and months, I found myself working through the aftermath of her attempted suicide. There was a lot of hurt between us that neither of us meant to inflict, and we were not equipped at that time to make a connection to begin healing or connecting to one another again.

The outward mess of untreated depression got messier as she refused to take antidepressants consistently. Watching her spiral into a deeper, darker hole - without any power to impact her in a positive way was one of the hardest times we ever had to walk through together.

But, time after time, when I wanted to scream (and sometimes did), break things, give up all hope, and walk away from everything, I would get a gentle reminder of the image of Jesus stepping backward, our hearts joining, and the blood pumping between us.

In the midst of what appeared to be a hopeless situation, a situation that felt like it was just a matter of time before I found my daughter dead, I would begin to fill up with a peace that made no sense in our circumstance. When I would get caught up in despair of what felt like losing my "Sweet Bee", slowly, worship would bring a fresh infusion of confidence in the truth that I am not doing things in my own strength, or alone. God resides within me and is for me.

There were really hard choices to make and actions to take that in the short term made me feel like I was a terrible mom and would never have close relationship with my daughter again. But they were actually actions I had to take to bring hope and potential life for her.

They were *hard*. Initially many of them caused more disunity between us, but I had to stop my role in her patterns of self-destruction. I had to stop trying to solve her problems and protect her from consequences of her choices. Through this season I really began to walk in the truth that I could do anything in a loving and hope filled way in *His* strength.

It took time, but our relationship is being restored and we are able to laugh and enjoy one another again. I am able to love her where she is, and let her be who she is, while still sharing wisdom, setting boundaries, and requiring her to commit to a few specific positive choices to continue receiving financial support while she is in school. We are learning to communicate clearly with love. I am thankful for the strength the Lord gave me, and continues to give me, as I pursue both of my children in more loving and purposeful relationships than I was able to in the past.

CHAPTER 9

SEEDS OF FAITH

I can still feel the long-ness of the journey from 1999 to 2016; those years were overflowing with really difficult life circumstance and events.

I was consumed with how I believed my husband did not love me at all, or love me well. I was filled with bitterness over what I lacked, and could not muster gratitude for the blessings in my life. I constantly compared myself to others – their bodies, their hair, their relationships, their jobs, their stuff, how clean their house was, how well they managed their time…

Much of my circumstances were simply consequences of my previous choices; some of them many years before I started following Jesus wholeheartedly. I often felt like I just could not catch a break. Things constantly went wrong, in ways I had not planned or prepared for. In all of it, I had to simply remind myself, however little actual belief there was inside me, that God would 'work this, too, for my good.' I may not see how until I got to heaven, but I chose to trust His promise over my feelings. When I stopped to consider 'then and now,' I was always able to see the dial had moved, sometimes in the smallest possible measurements, toward more abundant life and away from hopelessness.

There was a time during my separation and divorce process that I did not have enough money to pay the bills every month. At least not on paper. But somehow everything was always paid. There were other seasons in my life this was not the case, but during this particular time, there was consistent and miraculous provision to meet my needs, as well as money available to be generous to others.

The faith by which I had to walk during this time taught me to enjoy obedience to the voice of God, even if it did not make sense to me. It was a time of becoming familiar with Holy Spirit's wordless promptings and acting from a place of trusting that I am His sheep, I know His voice, and I am able to follow Him.

One Thursday evening at a local prayer house, the Lord spoke to me while the offering baskets were being passed around. Having paid my bills and filled my gas tank, there was $12 cash left in my wallet (and a few dollars in my bank account) until Friday a week later.

I had been contemplating what I would do with my little bit of 'mad money' as the offering basket passed by. As I felt the wicker scratch against the palm of my hand I immediately knew I was to put the $12 into the basket as an act of faith in God's provision. It created a lot of pressure inside. I wanted to spend this little bit of money on something for me. A lip gloss or new nail polish, maybe. I realized I had before me a purposeful choice to open my hands and lay down my control and desires in order to receive God's power and promises. I pulled the ten and two ones out of my wallet and dropped them in the basket. There was a little ache of self-pity as the wicker scratched my other palm and moved down the aisle, out of reach to change my mind. I somehow always chose to be all in with God, but over the years a mild but distinct bitterness developed where I believed the Lord was always asking me to give in tangible ways and receive only in spiritual ways. My prayers for others answered quickly and powerfully, while prayers for myself were always answered with, "It's coming" or "Soon."

The next week went by quickly and I found myself at the prayer house again for that weekly evening service. After a hectic day of contract negotiations and skipping lunch to get work done, I had driven straight from work to the prayer house. My stomach was growling, so I opened my bank app on my phone to see if I had left enough cash in my checking account to buy dinner.

I was stunned by the balance. Something must be wrong. What did I forget to pay? I opened the checking account to see the detail and was even more shocked to see a $1200 deposit to my account that very day from an unexpected source!

I heard the Lord say, "I am multiplying your seeds of faith 100 fold. Sometimes 1000. Test me."

Full of holy fear, I was nervous to test the Lord but was not going to argue. I did not know what to do though. I dug through my purse and found two dimes, all the cash I had access to, and dropped them in the basket. I sat and praised the Lord through the service but was more than a little stunned by what had had happened and wondered what He would do with my twenty cents.

The next morning I stepped around the front of my car parked in the driveway and began to weep. There was a $20 bill laying on the ground below the driver's door.

Immediately a voice said, "It's not about the money. It is about your faith!" There was an understanding deposited with the words.

Where I sow IN FAITH, there would be a harvest. It took a while for me to understand I can sow my faith negatively as well as positively. But in that moment I knew, beyond a shadow of a doubt, that all the prayers that had been put in my heart by the Lord would be answered. Part of Him making me good soil happened by NOT always meeting my expectations of timing, but always giving His good gifts in perfect time. He was firmly saying NOT YET to petitions I made from an impatient self-focused place.

I understood He had been, and was still working to answer my prayers from 1999 to heal every wound and break every prison.

I understood that all the good things He had shown me for His church, and the people who are family, whether they know it yet or not, will come to pass.

I simply need to keep sowing the seeds of faith He has given me ; walking where He leads. It does not always make sense to me, but I know His voice and my hope is to follow it to a place of bringing Him great glory, breaking the gates of hell, and leading many captives into the loving embrace of their savior, Jesus.

.

CHAPTER 10

A DIRECT PATH

In October 2015 I found myself being led to climb to the top of the mound of dirt the Town of Flower Mound is named after.

Four years earlier, God had gathered a small group of us to pray atop this little hill for unity, reconciliation and breakthrough in the world around us and particularly among followers of Jesus. It was the early days of the Lord teaching me that as one of His sheep, I hear His voice and am able to follow Him. *(John10:27)*

In 2011, however, I did not know the Bible very well. I kept being led in various actions and prayers that I believed were from the Lord, but didn't know how to test them against the scriptures or discern spirits as we are directed to do in the Bible.

A sweet gift of a friend, Jessica, was brought into my life. She seemed to always have a scripture address at her fingertips when I would tell her about the words I was hearing, pictures I was seeing, and sensations I was feeling. It was encouraging as well as inspiring! It was a life season full of adventure, laughter, and strong friendships being grown.

But, I had not thought about the Flower Mound in a very long time.

As I reached the top of the Mound, I turned slowly surveying the view. The drama, growth, and healing I had experienced ran through my mind like a movie on fast forward. My eyes focused on the dark blur in the distance and I realized I was seeing downtown Dallas the same way I would view it from the bedroom I had recently moved into in the Oak Lawn neighborhood. The difference being, my bedroom was 22 miles closer to downtown than where I currently stood. A weight began to settle in my heart, a sensation I have learned means the Lord is about to shift something deep within me.

I heard the words "It was a direct path from that day to this one."

I let out a breath, not realizing I had been holding it for some unknown amount of time.

I am a visual person so the picture before me really made space in my mind for those words to reach my heart.

It had not *felt* like a direct path from the Fall 2011 to Fall 2015. In those four years I had gone through a traumatic divorce, moved three times, gave everything I owned away twice, and walked through multiple tragedies in my family, including the death of my dad and my daughter's attempt to take her own life.

In those years I also grew greatly in understanding who I am because I am a believer in and follower of Jesus. I had put off old identity such as I am: worthless, stupid, clumsy, a waste of oxygen, a failure, and never good enough.

I had put on truth about myself in Jesus; that I am valuable just because He created me. I have a purpose that only I can fulfill, and that I am loved right now, even before I have gotten myself "all together," and have fixed all my faults.

I grew in His gifts to me; mercy, hospitality, teaching, prophecy, miraculous healings, and others.

In those four years, I had built many deep friendships and had been healed in ways I didn't expect.

I stood on "The Mound," feeling the edge of life before me, on the cusp of stepping into the destiny the Lord had not only been preparing me for, but had prepared for me.

The facts don't look or sound like a direct path. They look and sound a lot like a hot mess of a life, full of drama and more twists and turns than a soap opera.

But God.

The Lord knew where we were going. And through His grace, which is sufficient, I was able to do everything He asked me to do, everything I needed to do. Every moment was a step in, and toward, the destiny He has for me. Every moment was the Lord rebuilding me, after what I had built was torn down.

I could feel the closeness of this new thing the Lord had prepared. I was not sure what it would look like when it arrived. I had confidence in the 30,000 foot view, but not the minute details.

He had been faithful to bring me through the fires of life. People who knew me even five or six years earlier were amazed at the transformation in me.

The truth of the directness of the path encouraged me beyond words and strengthened me to walk much more boldly by faith and not by sight.

In Jesus, the best is always yet to come. It is beyond what we can even think to imagine to ask God to do in us, through us, or around us!

"Now unto him that is able to do exceeding abundantly above all that we ask or think, according to the power that works in us."
Ephesians 3:20 (KJV)

Dallas from the Mound   Dallas from apartment

CHAPTER 11

HOLY HUDDLE

The first time the Lord sent me to Upper Room Dallas was September 1, 2013. I was tired and cranky. There was a Texas thunderstorm brewing and the drive was a long one. Forty minutes one way.

By this time in my life, I had gained confidence that I was hearing the Lord's voice and discerning it from all others. I knew the Lord wanted me to attend the Sunday night service, but he had not told me why I was going.

At the time, it seemed rather uneventful. At one point, during corporate prayer for blessing and commissioning a couple going to Croatia, I saw a gentle rain in the spirit. One of the pastors stepped forward at the same moment, announcing they sensed the Lord was releasing healing in the room. While it was a sweet night, I did not readily see any particular reason for the Lord wanting me to be there.

The service ended and I went home without any expectation of ever returning.

But God. He works all things for the good of those who love Him, and does so beyond what we are capable of even imagining to ask.

God can do anything, you know — far more than you could ever imagine or guess or request in your wildest dreams! He does it not by pushing us around but by working within us, his Spirit deeply and gently within us. Ephesians 3:20 (MSG)

Three months later I found myself driving south on I35, headed to the Upper Room again. The location I originally attended had been shut down by the fire marshal. There were so many people crowding into the small room upstairs that the floor would dip and rise with the people as they moved during worship. Fortunately, their Sunday services had moved to a church next door.

I took a seat in the front left area of the room, the space I like to occupy during worship. As the first song began, I felt my heart quickly connect with the Lord's. I stretched out with my face on the floor and had a series of three visions over the next hour.

In the first vision, I saw myself standing in an open area; Father Son and Holy Spirit came to stand around me. They began to move around me in a circle that increased in speed until they fused into a blur of color and light before coming together over me, forming a shining, protective three section covering that swaddled me. I saw this image for a few moments before the three sections began to pull back and a thick strong tree trunk rose out of the now open triune-cocoon. When the tree trunk was quite tall, twelve branches began to grow from the center in a wheel-spoke formation, making the top of the tree flat from the side view. When the branches reached their full size each had a red juicy fruit sprout and grow at the end of it. The fruit resembled pomegranate seeds, but were the size of beach balls, or larger.

I sat up and grabbed my journal. As I sat on the pew, a second vision came to me. In this vision a tree appeared, and I heard the Lord say, "This is a fig tree." Then the vision ended.

In the last song of the evening, I was standing with my eyes lifted to heaven when I had a third vision. In it, I saw two trees growing up from the ground. One was a light wood and the other a dark wood, but both rich in color, healthy and with strong trunks. After they had grown about a third of their height, they began to wrap around one another as they continued to grow taller. As I looked I saw their canopies open to become lit menorahs.

Even though I could feel the significance of being there that evening, and I have the gift of interpretation of tongues and dreams, I needed help understanding what the Lord had given me during worship. I think it is purposeful of the Lord to keep us dependent on others. We are designed to function within community, and receiving interpretation from others is an amazing way to connect and build deep relationships. The three visions went on my prophetic shelf and would stay there for several months until I felt the Lord lead me to share with another.

In the early part of 2014, I attended one of John Paul Jackson's live recording sessions for Streams Ministry. During the time after taping ended, I felt led to share the three visions with him. His interpretations came instantly, but were very high level.

The first vision was the Lord showing me what He is going to do with me, His plan for me.

The second vision was the Lord saying it would be in His timing. Fig trees symbolically represent timing.

The third vision was the Lord letting me know that I could not fulfill His plan for me alone.

I was thankful for the new understanding, but still had more questions and had a familiar sense that I would have to wait for answers to come in the Lord's time. I journal extensively and keep many voice memos of the words, impressions, and experiences the Lord gives me. This has enabled me to go back and read or listen and understand how He takes His time to do good works. Sometimes months, other times years, but always perfect timing!

Over 2014 and 2015 the Lord would give me "assignments" to encourage and pray for people at the Upper Room. He would give me dates the assignments ended and each time one finished, I would ask Him to let me stay. I loved my home church but felt like I was *with my tribe* at the Upper Room.

Those two years were also some of the hardest I have ever personally walked through, but then it was time to step into a new thing. To begin to be the me that the Lord had been working to bring forth since 1999.

Starting in fall of 2015, the Lord had me give away almost everything I owned, move from my comfortable community in the suburbs to the heart of the city, leave my job of 11 years, leave my church home, and begin the process of stepping into the fruit of the previous 16 years.

There had been a great deal of destruction in the relationships with my daughter and son from when I was angry and bitter. Over the years I longed for and sought restoration with them. They always encouraged me that I had been a good mom, but it broke my heart and stretched my faith and hope at how slowly we seemed to be reconnecting. I wanted our life to be sunshine and roses everywhere, yesterday!

In the midst of all the change over the six months, there was a distinct breakthrough in mental strongholds and I began to live from a new place of who I am rather than what had happened to me and those I love. I saw the constant drama and turmoil in my life begin to turn into reconciliation and freedom for me and my family.

In April 2016, my pastor, Michael Miller, stood up to teach one Sunday and asked for three volunteers. He had them huddle up together and began to explain the way Father Son and Holy Spirit function as a whole, while remaining three unique persons. He moved into teaching on 'the day of trouble.'

Pastor Miller asked for a fourth volunteer and sat them in the middle of the huddle. He began to explain how, in the day of trouble, this is where we are to be. When we rest in that place, the holy huddle, we are carried through the day of trouble and into the new mercies of the morning.

As I sat there I recalled the first vision I had at Upper Room and how I had seen the Trinity wrap around me. My heart was full of thankfulness. I realized I had been taken to and kept in that place of safety and love among the Trinity, and that the Lord had done that through showing me each tiny step as it needed to be taken. I remained in that place because I continued to give Him my "yes."

I was cared for and protected so well by pastors, elders, and staff during my 8 ½ years at The Village Church. Through the Recovery and Steps ministry, I healed from much of my past and learned to assess my own heart posture in situations so that I am better positioned to take rogue thoughts captive. I learned who God says He is in His written word. I was given the opportunity to exercise my gifts and grow in a place where I felt safe and confident that my pastors and friends would be there to help me if I got tripped up while prophesying, praying for healing, or exercising other gifts as Holy Spirit made them available to me.

My personal spiritual, emotional, and character growth during 2014 and 2015 had been ridiculously fast. Attributable in large part to what the Lord was doing, and my pastor Michael Miller was partnering with, at the Upper Room. There are many hours of prayer and worship inviting Holy Spirit to rest in that place and we draw near to Him as scripture encourages. My personal hours spent there in in the presence of our living God were an incubator for my spirit to flourish. It was not a space strategically created, but circumstantially birthed from many people coming together genuinely seeking to bless the Lord with all their heart and soul.

"But God chose the foolish things of the world to shame the wise; God chose the weak things of the world to shame the strong." 1 Corinthian 1:17 (NIV)

On April Fool's Day 2016 I began to write this book, and I believe it is the first evidence of the fruit I saw on the tree trunks in the first vision. There is not a purpose or target audience other than being faithful to share what the Lord has asked me to share. I trust it will reach and bless exactly who He had in mind when He birthed this in my heart to create.

I continue to sit in that place of safety among the Trinity. I have come to understand the ways I have been designed to connect with the Lord's heart, which are not the same as everyone else's, even when they are similar. I pursue those connections with God and joyfully pay the cost to receive the blessing of living in His presence.

Loving the Lord our God with all our heart, mind, and soul is a beautiful mess. He brings the beauty; we bring the mess. I invite you to join me there. It will be a journey. It will be hard at times and amazingly easy at others. There will be tears and fists shaken at the Lord as well as shouts of victory and praise. There will be heartbreak and disappointment, because those things are part of this broken world we live in. But you can find the secret place where the Lord meets you, where He fills you and sustains you. I invite you to jump into the deep things of God with Holy Spirit to see His perfect beauty and the unique way you are exquisitely, uniquely beautiful in His sight.

Cover Art "Becoming" painting and poem by Michelle Sims

EMERGING
        no longer invisible
BECOMING
        me, myself, and I
LONGING
        for truth and justice
JESUS
        come bring me to life